Wacky World

Smarties Wacky World

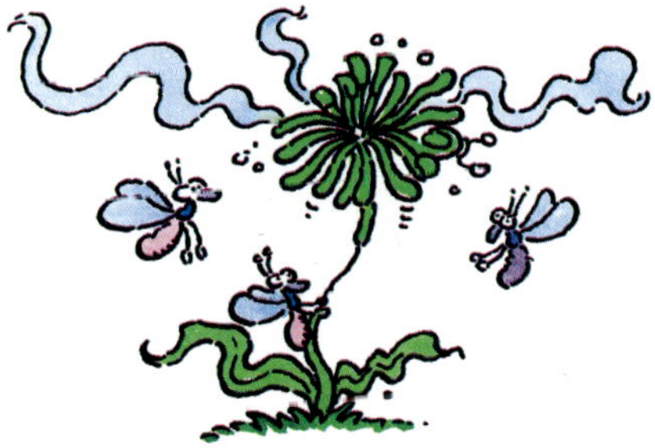

text by Mike Ashley

illustrations by David Mostyn

Robinson Children's Books

First published in the UK by Robinson Children's Books,
an imprint of Constable & Robinson Ltd, 2001

Constable & Robinson Ltd
3 The Lanchesters
162 Fulham Palace Road
London W6 9ER
www.constablerobinson.com

Text © Mike Ashley
Illustrations © David Mostyn 2001
Typeset and coloured by Oxford Designers & Illustrators
Edited by Sue Nicholson

NESTLÉ and SMARTIES are registered trademarks of
Société des Produits Nestlé S.A., 1800 Vevey, Switzerland.
© 2001 Société des Produits Nestlé S.A., 1800 Vevey, Switzerland.
Trade Mark Owners.

All rights reserved. This book is sold subject to the condition
that it shall not, by way of trade or otherwise, be lent, resold,
hired out or otherwise circulated in any form of binding or
cover other than that in which it is published and without a
similar condition being imposed on the subsequent purchaser.

A copy of the British Library Cataloguing in Publication Data
for this title is available from the British Library.

ISBN 1 84119 408 5

10 9 8 7 6 5 4 3 2 1

Contents

Welcome to this wacky world — 6—7

What on Earth!? — 8—27
Staggering facts about Planet Earth;
awesome oceans, exploding mountains,
shuddering earthquakes and much more.

What's out there? — 28—41
The most amazing facts about outer space –
the stars, planets and the Universe.

Spectacular science — 42—53
The mind-boggling wacky world of science.
From the smelliest smells to the weirdest
inventions.

Mysterious X-Files — 54—67
Super-spooky facts about ghosts, monsters
and other unknown weird stuff!

Fun and games — 68—85
This is where the fun really starts, with
hundreds of incredible facts and figures
about sports, games and entertainment.

Oddities and entities — 86—95
A few things that were just too odd to ignore.

Index — 96

WELCOME TO THIS WACKY WORLD

If you didn't know that we live in a wacky world, in a wacky galaxy, in an even wackier universe, then you're about to find out!

This book is crammed with amazing and awesome facts and finds out why our home is such a beautiful, mysterious and funny place to live.

You'll learn about the powerful forces of nature, and the biggest, smallest, fastest and strangest things in the world.

There's some spectacular science and super-spooky stories about ghosts and monsters. Plus lots of incredible facts and figures about sports, games and entertainment.

You can even zoom into outer space to look at the planets, asteroids and black holes!

Have fun!

Mike Ashley.

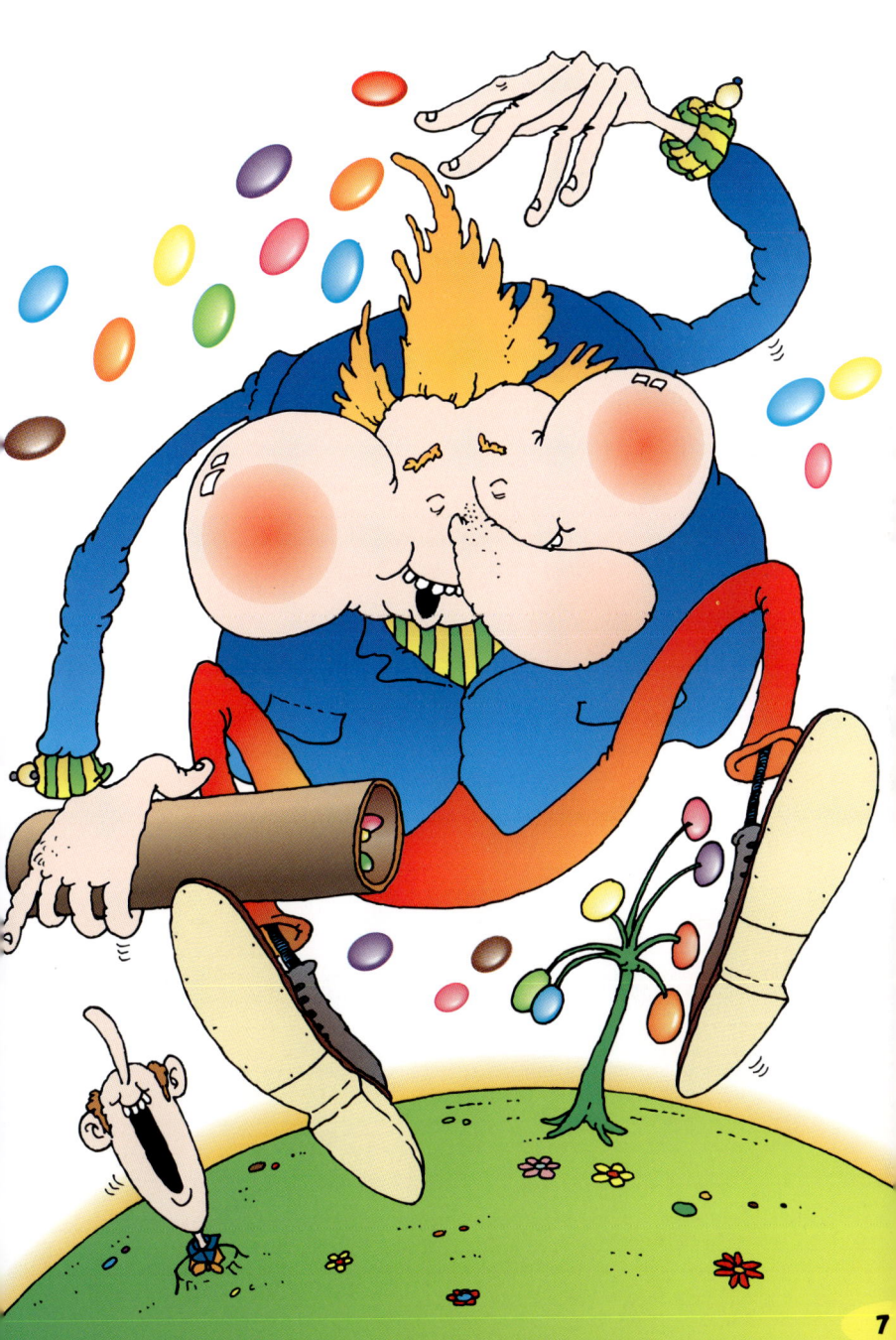

WHAT ON EARTH!?

Earth is our home, and it's a wonderfully diverse and beautiful place. It's full of mountains, lakes, seas, deserts, forests and so much more, making it a great place to explore.

Of all the planets, Earth is the only one that has an abundance of water. In fact there's so much water the planet should be called Water not Earth.

It's the only planet, so far as we know, that supports life. It's an amazing world, but also a fragile one. In this section we'll look at many of the wonderful things about the natural world and at some of the scary things.

You'll find out:

- the furthest you can go – up, down and roundabout
- the hottest and coldest places
- where it's wettest and driest
- the most dangerous places
- the biggest seaside
- the greatest waves
- the worst weather

. . . and a lot more.

Weighty matters

The Earth weighs a staggering 5,976 sextillion kg. Suppose you could dump the Earth on one side of a set of scales. To equal it on the other side you'd need to place:

- 1.15 quadrillion Great Pyramids of Egypt; or
- 80 Moons

If you wanted to walk all the way around the equator you'd have to walk 40,075km. At normal walking speed it would take you 346 days non-stop. Mind you, you'd get very wet as most of the time you'd be under water!

Gulp

The Earth may be big, but the Sun could swallow up 1,303,600 Earths.

Where do we all live?

The total land surface of the Earth is 149.2 million sq km. But that's only 29% of the whole surface – the rest is water.

Sardines

Though you might think that the Earth is crawling with people, we're actually all crammed on to less than 12% of the Earth's surface – the bits that aren't covered in water, ice, desert or jungle.

Just islands

All the land on Earth is surrounded by water, though we don't usually think of the bigger chunks as islands.

The biggest land mass is Eurasia (the continents of Europe and Asia). This covers 53,697,000 sq km or about 36% of the Earth's land surface.

Two of the other continents are really large islands. Antarctica is 14,250,000 sq km – that's 64 times bigger than Britain – and Australia is 7,618,493 sq km.

The next biggest island is Greenland which is 2,175,600 sq km, nearly 10 times bigger than Britain.

Beside the seaside

The total length of the coastline around all the continents and islands in the world is 848,000km. This is further than the distance from the Earth to the Moon and back again.

The longest coastline of any country is Canada's, which is 243,791km long. Unfortunately, much of it is frozen for most of the year, so it's not a good place for a long-distance paddle.

The country with the shortest coastline is Monaco, which is less than 4km, but it's also the richest, with millions of pounds worth of yachts moored there.

Far away from anywhere

The most remote island in the world is Bouvet Island. No one lives here. It's 1,700km from the nearest neighbour, which is also uninhabited – Antarctica. The nearest people are over 2,000km away on the tiny island of Tristan da Cunha, which is the most remote island where people live.

GET THIS!

The most populated and noisiest island in the world is Hong Kong. Not the place for getting away from it all!

Cliffs and canyons

The island of Molokai, in Hawaii, has cliffs over 1,005m high. They're nearly 6 times higher than the famous cliffs at Beachy Head on the English south coast.

The Grand Canyon in Arizona is the largest chasm in the world. It is
- over 349km long
- up to 20km wide
- down to 2,133m deep.

Although not as long as the Grand Canyon, Hell's Canyon in Oregon and Idaho is the deepest. The Snake River flows 2400m below the towering cliffs of Devil Mountain.

Gigantic waves

Ordinary waves are caused by the wind. The highest natural wave ever spotted was 34m from trough to crest. This was in the Pacific Ocean during a hurricane in 1933.

Earthquakes or volcanic explosions also cause waves. These are called tsunamis. The highest recorded tsunami was 85m high, or twice the height of Nelson's Column. The fastest recorded tsunami was travelling at 900km/h.

How far down can you go?

The deepest ocean is the Pacific. At its deepest point it goes down to 11,022m. This is in the Marianas Trench near the island of Guam. This trench is so deep it would swallow Mount Everest.

The Marianas Trench is far deeper than the deepest known caves which are the Reseau Jean Bernard in France. They only go down 1,602m.

Highest heights

How far can you go up and still be on land?

Mount Everest (also called Chumulongma) at 8,846m is usually called the highest mountain in the world. But it isn't! It's the highest point above sea level.

The tallest mountain in the world is Mauna Kea, a Hawaiian volcano that measures 10,206m from bottom to top. However, $3/5$ of it (6,000m) are under water. It's as high as almost 27 Empire State Buildings or 181 Nelson's Columns.

GET THIS!

Where on Earth is furthest from the centre of the Earth?

The Earth bulges at the equator because it spins. So it's possible for a tall mountain near the equator to have a peak further from the centre of the Earth than Everest. The top of Mount Chimborazo in Ecuador is 2,150m further from the centre of the Earth than the top of Everest.

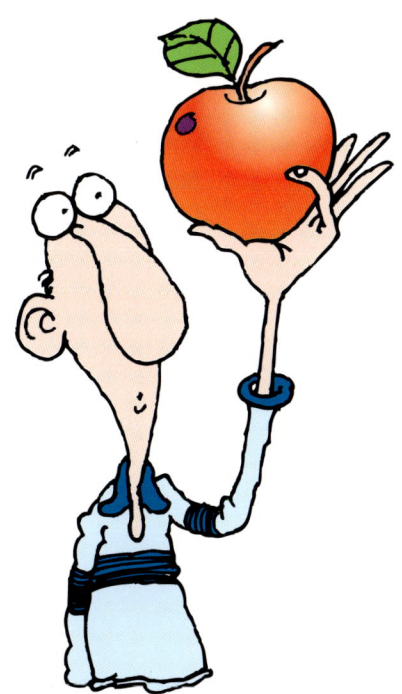

Under your feet

What is under the surface of the Earth?

The distance to the centre of the Earth is about 6,360km, which is about the same as the distance across the United States from New York to Los Angeles. It doesn't seem very far, but the journey would be hard to make, solid in fact.

First you'd have to get through the Earth's crust. This is solid rock between 5 and 35km thick.

If the Earth were the size of an apple, the crust would be equal to the apple's skin.

Below the crust is the Earth's mantle. The further down you go the hotter it gets. The rocks start to turn to jelly and then melt into liquid rock, the same as lava that spews out of volcanoes.

At a depth of 5,000km, you enter the Earth's core. Here the temperature is 6,000°C. That's hotter than the surface of the Sun.

Drifting continents

Believe it or not the continents are still moving at about 3cm a year – or 12 times slower than your fingernails grow. Over 65 million years this is equal to 1,950km!

Making mountains

Mountains are formed by upward movements and folding of the Earth's rocky crust. This happens because the continents are still moving. When India bumped into Asia the land in between buckled and the Himalayas were formed.

Soggiest mountains

The highest mountain that is totally covered by water is an unnamed peak in the Tonga Trench just south of Tonga in the Pacific. It is 8,690m high, and its peak is 365m below the surface of the sea.

The Mid-Atlantic Ridge, the world's longest mountain range, is entirely under water. It runs all the way down the centre of the Atlantic Ocean. It's 11,300km long, which is much longer than the longest mountain range on land. This is the Andes in South America, which is 7,242km long.

Exploding mountains

When a volcano explodes it throws ash, rocks and dust into the sky. Molten rock (called lava) spurts out and flows down the mountain side like a red-hot river.

The world's highest volcano is Aconcagua in the Andes. It is 6,960m high, but has not erupted for millions of years.

The highest active volcano is Guallatiri, in Chile, which is 6,060m high. The last time it erupted was in 1959.

The most famous volcano is probably Mount Vesuvius in Italy. In AD 79 it erupted, and the lava buried the towns of Pompeii and Herculaneum in mud and rocks over 18m deep. Vesuvius is one of the world's most dangerous volcanoes, because so many people live near it.

The biggest bangs

The loudest volcanic eruption of recent times happened in Indonesia on the island of Krakatoa in 1883. The explosion hurled rocks 55km into the air. The sound of it was heard up to 4,800km away. The eruption caused a tidal wave over 41m high.

Edinburgh Castle is built on the core of an extinct volcano.

The island of Surtsey suddenly appeared in 1963 off the coast of Iceland. It was formed by an undersea volcano.

The eruption of Santorini on the island of Thira in the Aegean Sea, near Greece, in 1470 BC destroyed the civilization of Crete. It left behind beaches of black ash – imagine playing on a beach of coal dust. I bet it gets pretty hot in the sun.

Droughting deserts

We think of deserts as hot, dry, sandy places, but a desert is any waste land where scarcely anything grows. The world's biggest desert is the Antarctic. Although 98% of its surface is permanently covered with ice, the rest is barren rock.

The largest hot desert is the Sahara in North Africa. It covers 8,400,000 sq km – it's about 16 times the size of France.

The driest desert in the world is the Atacama in Chile, South America – there are parts where it hasn't rained for hundreds of years. So remember to take a drink with you.

Shuddering shocks

Earthquakes happen when pressures build up and cause the Earth's crust to suddenly buckle and shift. Most earthquakes last for only a second or two, but the San Francisco earthquake of 1906 lasted for 47 seconds.

Believe it or not there are even earthquakes in Britain. The biggest known happened in 1931 on the Dogger Bank in the North Sea. It reached level 6. Bet that shook the fish up a lot!

GET THIS!

If records are to be believed the worst earthquake of all happened in Syria and northern Egypt during the Crusades in 1201. Over 1 million people were killed.

Mr Richter

The strength of an earthquake is measured on a scale invented by Charles Richter in 1935 and called the Richter Scale. It goes from 0 to 9, and each level is 10 times stronger than the previous level. Level 9 is over 40,000 times more powerful than the atomic bomb dropped on Hiroshima.

Counting quakes

There are half a million earthquakes a year, but only about 1 in 500 causes damage. About 100 of these are level 6 quakes, 20 are level 7 quakes and 1 or 2, level 8 quakes.

Big shakes

The most powerful earthquake was in Japan in 1933. It reached level 8.9 and killed 2,990 people. Only 10 years before, a level 8.3 quake in Japan killed 143,000 people.

Awesome oceans

Of the four major oceans – the Pacific, the Atlantic, the Indian and the Arctic – the Pacific is the biggest. It covers over 179.6 million sq km. That's more than all the land on the Earth's surface.

The oceans contain about 1,377 quintillion litres of water. If that were shared out among every person on Earth we would each have 8.2 million litres for every day of our life. That's enough for over 105,000 baths every day!

GET THIS!

The sea contains traces of gold. There are 4g in every billion kg of seawater, or over 5 billion kg of gold in total. It's so diluted it's not worth the huge cost of extraction.

Raging rivers

Rivers account for only 0.028% of all the fresh water on the planet, but this still amounts to about 10.5 quadrillion litres.

The longest river in the world is the Nile, at 6,670km. There's another river flowing deep underground below the Nile and it holds 6 times more water than the Nile.

Luscious lakes

It's all very well having all that sea water, but we can't drink it. We need fresh water. Only 2.6% of all the world's water is fresh.

Very salty

Not all lakes are fresh water. The Caspian Sea is really a lake because it's entirely surrounded by land. It's nearly 12 times the size of Lake Baikal. But it's full of salt water.

GET THIS!

The Dead Sea, on the border of Israel and Jordan, is so full of salt that it is 16% more dense than fresh water, making it impossible for anyone to sink in it. So you don't need armbands when you're learning to swim.

The world's wettest lakes

Lake Baikal in Russia wins the prize for the deepest lake – it's over 1.6km deep.
Let's take a look at the 5 biggest freshwater lakes in the world.

Lake	Surface area (*square km*)	Volume (trillion gallons)	% of World's lakes & rivers
Baikal	31,494	5,069	14.1%
Tanganyika	32,900	4,021	11.2%
Superior	82,100	2,674	7.5%
Malawi/Nyasa	28,879	1,348	3.8%
Michigan	57,800	1,080	3.0%

Hot water

Geysers are like giant pressure cookers – superheated steam and water are thrown out of the ground in explosive jets. The highest natural geyser in the world is the Steamboat Geyser in the Yellowstone National Park in Wyoming, USA. It ejects water to a height of 115m.

Amazing Amazon

The Amazon holds the most water. On average the river contains about 1,360 trillion litres.

Incredibly, if the second and third longest rivers, the Amazon and the Yangtze-Kiang, were placed end to end, they would reach almost exactly from the North Pole to the South Pole through the centre of the Earth.

Rivers are at their most dangerous when they flood. Yet farmers in Egypt rely on the Nile flooding every year to bring water and nutrients to their fields. Without these floods there would have been no Egyptian civilization and no Pyramids.

Flood warning

The most dangerous river for flooding is the Hwang-He or Yellow River, known as China's Sorrow. The worst ever flood happened in 1931 when over 3,700,000 people died.

Aaaaah!

There are at least five rivers in the world with the name Aa. Pretty obvious name for a river if you stumble across it in the dark.

The big splash

The highest waterfall in the world is the Angel Falls in south-east Venezuela, but it's really no more than a runny nose! What water there is plummets down 978m. That's $3\frac{1}{4}$ times the height of the Eiffel Tower in Paris.

Stunning

The most spectacular waterfalls are the Boyoma (or Stanley) Falls in the Democratic Republic of the Congo, Africa. Over 16.8 million litres of water flow over those falls every second.

Going going gone

The Guairá Falls between Brazil and Paraguay used to beat the Boyoma hands down, with over 50 million litres of water flowing over them every second. However, with the building of the Itaipú Dam in 1982, the Falls vanished under the waters.

Great atmosphere

The Earth's atmosphere extends up to about 900km, but the bit that we breathe and affects us with its weather is very small. It's called the troposphere. This rises to about 15km at the equator but only 8km at the poles.

The temperature of the troposphere falls by about 5°C for every 1,000 metres you rise above sea level.

The average daytime surface temperature of the Earth is about 15°C.

The top of Mount Everest is about −30°C.

The top of the troposphere is about −55°C.

GET THIS!

Every year humankind chucks over a trillion kg of pollutants into the atmosphere. That's over 3 times the weight of everyone on Earth.

Soggy statistics

There are about 483 billion kg of water vapour in the atmosphere. If it all fell as rain in one go it would cover the United States to a depth of 7.5m.

A single storm cloud may weigh as much as 500 million kg, so never underestimate a rainy day!

GET THIS!
The rainiest day ever recorded was 16 March 1952, when 1.8m fell on Réunion Island in the Indian Ocean.

Take a raincoat when you go to Mount Wai'ale'ale on Kauai in Hawaii. It rains there for 350–60 days every year, more than anywhere else on Earth.

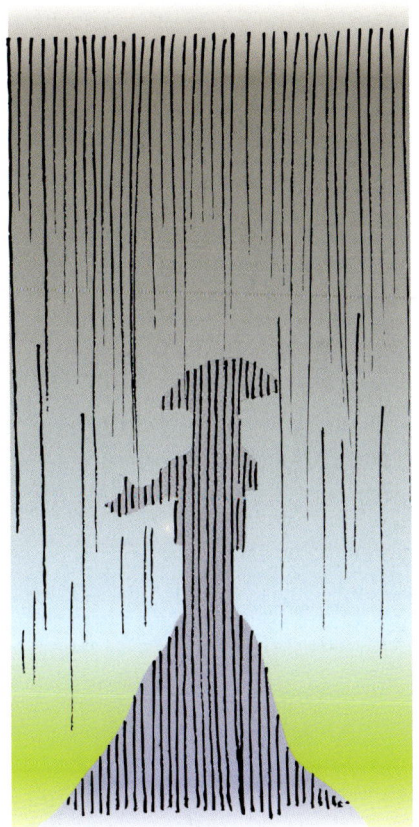

Hot and cold

The extremes of temperature between different places on Earth is astounding. Take a look at these awesome examples.

	Place (year)	Temperature
Hottest ever	Al' Azizyah, Libya (1922)	57.7°C
Hottest all-year average	Dallol, Ethiopia	34°C
Coldest ever	Vostock, Antarctica (1983)	–89.2°C
Coldest all-year average	Plateau Station, Antarctica	–57°C
Coldest village	Oymyakon, Siberia	–72°C

Lightning strikes

As you're reading this there are about 2,000 thunderstorms occurring all over the Earth. There are over 8 million lightning strikes every day.

How far?

If you count the number of seconds after seeing lightning, until you hear the thunder, then for every 2 seconds the storm is about 1 km away.

Lightning strikes can reach awesome speeds of 50,000–140,000km per second – *that's almost half the speed of light!*

Between 1942 and 1977 Roy Sullivan, a park ranger in Virginia, USA, was struck by lightning 7 times yet survived.

Windy worries

Have you ever felt the wind blow so strongly you thought you'd be blown away? The strongest winds occur in tornadoes – the fastest yet recorded was 450km/h at Wichita Falls in Texas in 1958.

The windiest place in the world is in the Antarctic where there are gales raging at over 175km/h for many months of the year. At least it's not as windy as it is on Neptune.

Hotting up

The Earth is gradually warming up. This steady increase is believed to be due to the 'greenhouse effect' – where heat is trapped inside the atmosphere owing to a build-up of carbon dioxide.

Freezing facts

A single snowflake weighs as little as one-thousandth of a gram, and yet the total amount of fresh snow that falls each year in the whole world weighs 450 trillion kg. That's trillions of snowflakes and yet it's believed that no two snowflakes ever look the same.

The largest snowflakes that have ever fallen were 38cm across and 20cm thick. They fell at Fort Keogh, Montana on 28 January 1887.

A single snow cloud can drop up to 41 billion kg of snow.

The most snow to fall on 1 day was 1.9m at Silver Lake, Colorado, in April 1921.

More snow falls on Canada than on any other country in the world – an ideal place to hold a snowman building competition?

GET THIS!

A few years ago a lorry driver stopped in Oymyakon in Siberia and, not realizing how cold it was, got out of his cab – within seconds he had frozen to the spot.

Frozen solid

80% of the world's fresh water is frozen as ice, snow or permafrost.

Super stars

The most stars you can see in one go, without a telescope, is about 2,500 – but that's nothing compared with the total number of stars in the Universe.

Our solar system is just a small part of one galaxy, which we call the Milky Way. Our galaxy contains about 100 billion stars. If each star were the size of a grain of rice, this number would fill a cathedral.

In total there are estimated to be around 100 billion galaxies, each with about the same number of stars. That's a total of 10 sextillion stars or 10,000,000,000,000,000,000,000. And that's probably on the low side!

Nearest star

The nearest star to Earth is our Sun. It's about 150 million km away. Light from the Sun takes 8 minutes 19 seconds to reach us.

Next nearest star

The next nearest star is Proxima Centauri which is so far away that light takes 4.25 years to reach us – so we say it is 4.25 light-years away.

GET THIS!

The greatest speed possible is the speed of light. It travels at 300,000km per second. A light-year is the distance light travels in 1 year. This is equal to 9,458,688 million km.

Supersonic

If you could fly into space directly by Concorde, it would take 7.3 years to get to the Sun, but it would take nearly 2 million years to reach Proxima Centauri.

Biggest and brightest

The brightest star you can see in the night sky is Sirius. It is about 26 times brighter than the Sun, but appears less bright because it is further away. As stars go, it's actually quite close, about 8.64 light-years. You can find Sirius by looking at the constellation of Orion and following the belt of Orion down to the left.

The brightest known star in our galaxy is Eta Carinae, which is as bright as 6 million of our Suns. It's about 6,400 light-years away. About 100 years ago it was one of the brightest stars in the sky, but since then it has become surrounded by space dust and is now hidden from the naked eye.

Most distant stars

The furthest known stars from the Earth are in the remotest known galaxy of all. The galaxy doesn't yet have a name, and was only discovered in 1997. The light reaching us from these stars left them 13 billion years ago, which was soon after the Universe was created, and long before the Earth was formed.

Space travel

But say you leapt into the fastest spaceship there is and zoomed off beyond our solar system. How long would it take you to reach some of those fantastic stars, going at a cool 112km per second?

	Distance in Light-years	*How long to get there (years)*
Proxima Centauri	4.25	18,000
Sirius	8.64	37,000
Betelgeuse	650	2.78 million
Eta Carinae	6,400	27.3 million
Nearest galaxy	80,000	213 million
Furthest you can see without a telescope (the Andromeda Spiral)	2,200,000	9.4 billion
Furthest known galaxy	13,000,000,000	55.5 trillion
Edge of Universe	Over 14,000,000,000	60 trillion

Can you see it?

The biggest star you can see in the sky is Betelgeuse (pronounced 'bet-el-jeuz'). You'll find it in the top left corner of Orion. Betelgeuse has a diameter of 1 billion km, which is 718 times wider than our Sun.

Miles and miles away

Everything about the Universe is massive and everything in it is a long way away.

Mercury is closer to the Sun than we are, but it's still 57.9 million km from it, and light from the Sun takes 3 minutes to reach it.

Pluto, the most distant planet from the Sun, is 5,913.5 million km away. The Sun's light takes 5.5 hours to get there.

That's a mere hop and a skip compared with the distance from the Sun to the Oort Cloud (home of the distant comets). It takes 577 days for the Sun's light to reach the Oort Cloud, which is 15 trillion km away.

GET THIS!

The temperature at the centre of the Sun is an incredible 15 million°C.

Dead stars and black holes

Stars do eventually die. They burn off all their fuel leaving behind an extremely dense core called a neutron star. If the star was big, the core may have a pull of gravity so great that light cannot escape from it. When this happens it becomes a black hole. A black hole is not really a hole, but a point of super-gravity from which nothing can escape.

Black holes are the most dangerous places in the Universe. If you get too close to one you'll be crushed right out of existence.

Big Bang

You may have heard of the Big Bang. It's how most scientists think the Universe began. The Big Bang wasn't like an explosion, but was a sudden expansion, as if a balloon was being inflated at a terrific speed.

The Universe may come to an end one day, and maybe all that will be left is a black hole from which a new Universe may one day erupt, just like our own did with the Big Bang. But don't worry, this won't happen for billions and billions of years.

Sunny and bright

The Sun is a star. You should never look directly at it because it is so bright it could damage your eyes, even if you are wearing sunglasses. It is 600,000 times brighter than the full Moon.

The Sun is a massive ball of hot gas. It's the most massive object in the solar system by far – you could fit 1,303,600 Earths inside it. In fact it contains 99.8% of the total mass of the solar system.

The pressure at the centre of the Sun is immense. It is about 10 billion times the surface pressure on Earth.

Hot stuff

The temperature on the 'surface' of the Sun (the visible area we see) is a cool 5,500°C. Some parts of the surface are even cooler, about 4,000°C, and these look darker and are called sunspots. Some sunspots are huge – as much as 100,000km wide, or 8 times the diameter of the Earth.

Above the visible surface it's even hotter, and in the corona (the Sun's atmosphere, which you see during a total eclipse of the Sun), the temperature is as high as 2 million°C.

GET THIS!

You may think you're sitting still, but really you're moving at a terrific speed. The Earth is spinning on its axis at 1,670km/h. The Earth is moving around the Sun at 107,160km/h. And then we are moving with the Sun around the centre of the galaxy at 792,000km/h.

Stupendous speed

Speed in space is awesome. Remember that space is virtually a vacuum so there's nothing to stop objects moving at a high speed.

Full Moon

Astronomers believe that the Moon was created when a massive object hit the Earth when it was still forming and threw a huge chunk of molten rock into space where it cooled and became the Moon.

The Moon always presents the same face to the Earth. No one knew what the other side of the Moon looked like until the Russian spacecraft *Luna 3* sent back photographs in 1959.

The Moon is one of the slowest objects in the solar system. It travels only 1.6 times faster than Concorde.

Moonastery

The Moon has no atmosphere. So everything that happens on the Moon, even the impact of a meteorite, happens in complete silence. There are no winds, so everything on the Moon's surface remains undisturbed unless bombarded from space. The footprints left by the astronauts who walked on the Moon over 30 years ago are still there.

Extreme survival

The temperature on the Moon's surface varies from 117°C at noon to −163°C at night. No human could survive those extremes.

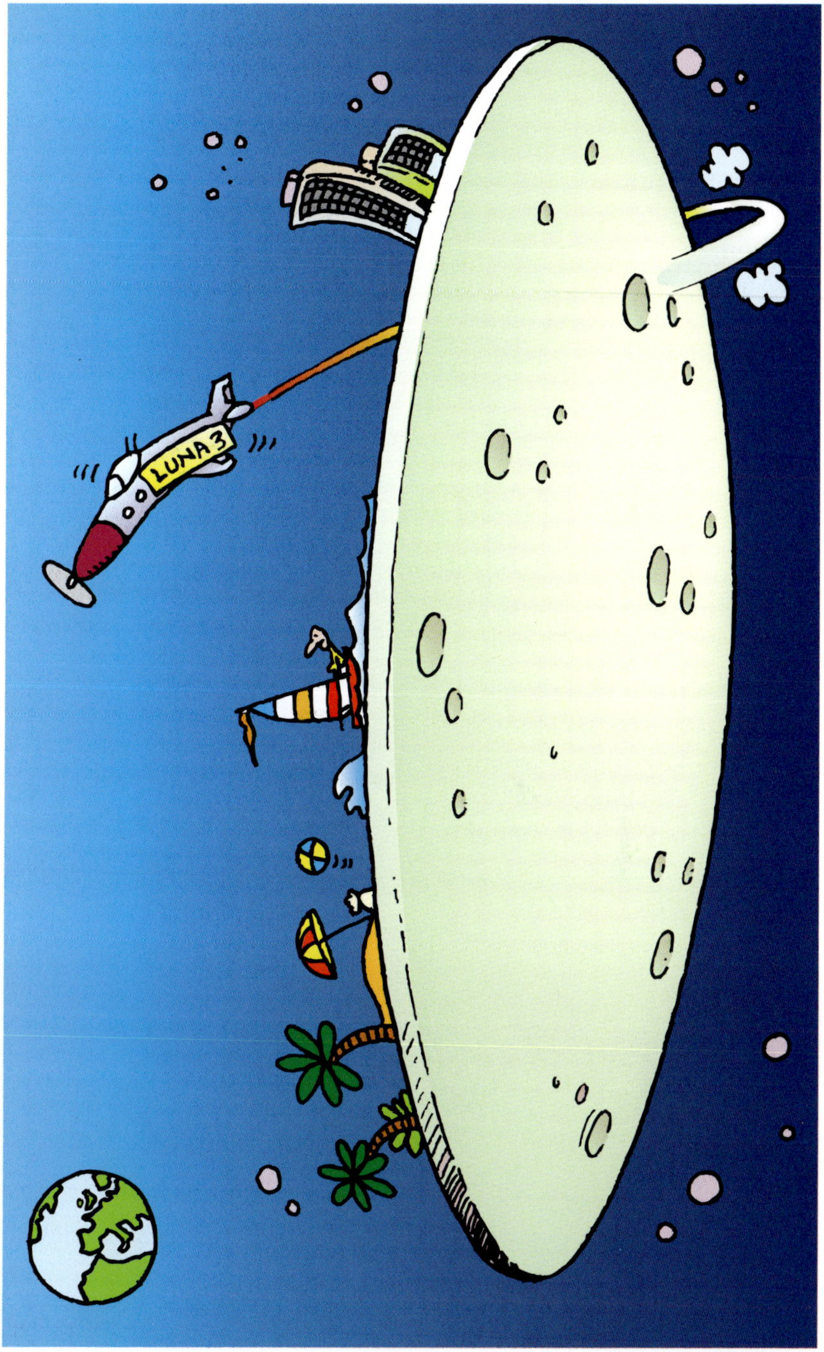
LUNA 3

THE PLANETS

The Earth is just one of nine major planets known to orbit the Sun. Let's have a look at some of the others.

Mercury

Mercury is the closest planet to the Sun. It has the most extreme temperatures of any planet, ranging from 427°C by day to –183°C at night.

Mercury has a very long day, which lasts for 59 Earth days – your Mum could not say 'there just are not enough hours in a day!' if she lived on Mercury.

Mercury's surface is pitted with craters like the Moon. It has no life, there is no sound, and little has changed on the surface for over 3,000 million years.

Venus

Venus is surrounded by dense poisonous clouds. No one knew what the surface looked like until pictures were sent back by the Russian space probe *Venera 9* in 1975.

Venus is the hottest planet in the solar system. The temperature on the surface is always about 460°C.

The intense heat, the suffocating air pressure, and the burning acid rain make the surface of Venus the most hostile place in the solar system, so don't book any holidays there.

A day on Venus is equal to 243 Earth days. Because Venus orbits the Sun in 225 days it means its day is longer than its year.

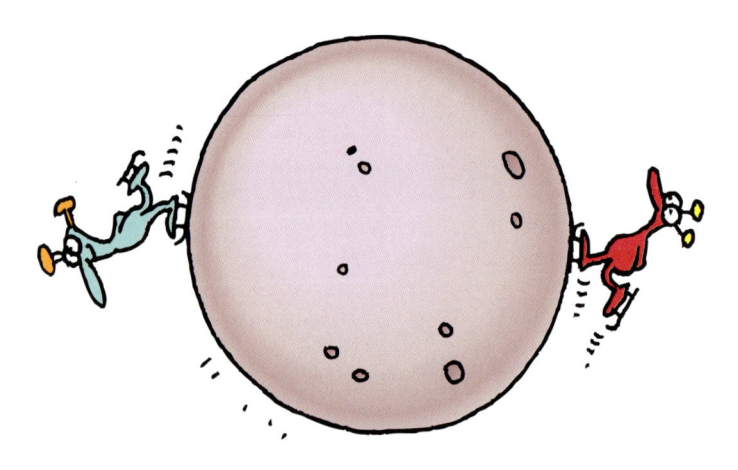

Mars

Mars is known as the Red Planet – its surface is rich in rusted iron, which makes it look red.

Mars has the largest volcano so far found in the solar system, called Olympus Mons. It is 24km high – 3 times higher than Mount Everest.

Mars has one of the deepest valleys in the solar system. The Valles Marineris is up to 7km deep, 600km wide and 4,000km long.

Mars has an atmosphere, but it's almost all carbon dioxide.

There is no liquid water on the surface, but there is ice at the poles.

The surface temperature ranges from 26°C in the day to as low as –110°C at night, so the average temperature is always below freezing. It's like a permanent Arctic.

Mars has two tiny moons – Phobos and Deimos. Phobos is so small, that in just over a kilometre you could walk from the day side where the temperature is like a winter's day in Scotland (about –4°C) to the night side, which is like Antarctica (–122°C).

Jupiter

Jupiter is the biggest planet in the solar system. It could swallow over 1,300 Earths – in fact it's bigger than all the other planets put together, twice over!

Jupiter is a gas giant – most of the planet is made up of gas, not rock like the Earth. It has a small rocky core, surrounded by a vast ocean of liquid hydrogen, thousands and thousands of kilometres deep.

The atmosphere on Jupiter stinks. It is made up of ice crystals of ammonia, methane and water.

The best known feature in Jupiter's atmosphere is called the Great Red Spot, which isn't named after your zits! It's probably the vortex of a giant hurricane about the same size as the Earth. This storm has been raging for at least the last 350 years.

Jupiter has 16 moons. One of them, Io, is covered by volcanoes that are constantly erupting. The lava from these volcanoes is hotter than anything in the solar system outside the Sun. It reaches temperatures of up to 1,700°C. Yet away from these volcanoes the temperature remains far below freezing.

Saturn

Saturn is the second largest planet, and another gas giant. It is far less dense than Jupiter, and would in fact float on water (if you could find enough!).

Saturn is renowned for its rings. They are made up of millions of tiny rocks, some as small as grains of sand, but others as large as 10m across.

It has at least 18 moons. One of them, Titan, is the second largest moon in the solar system.

GET THIS!

Titan is the likeliest place in our solar system, outside Earth, for life to develop. The surface is bitterly cold (about −170°C), but it could be that in millions of years, when our Sun grows old, the extra heat given out (which will destroy the Earth) might help life develop on Titan.

Uranus

Uranus is unusual in two ways. It is tipped over on its side, so it rolls around in orbit. Also, it spins the opposite way round to all the other planets.

Uranus is a gas giant like Jupiter but is much smaller – though it is still as big as 67 Earths.

Neptune

Neptune, another gas giant, is almost the same size as Uranus.

Its atmosphere is torn apart by the strongest winds in the solar system, blowing at up to 2,200km/h – about as fast as Concorde flies.

Pluto

Pluto is the furthest planet known. It was not discovered until 1930.

Pluto is so distant that it takes 248 Earth years to orbit the Sun once. That means it hasn't done one complete orbit since it was discovered.

Pluto is the smallest planet, and is even smaller than our own Moon. Some astronomers think it is too small to be a proper planet but is simply a large asteroid.

Comets

Far out in the depths of space beyond Pluto's orbit is the home of the comets. Maybe as many as 200 billion small rocks and planetoids orbit the Sun out there. Occasionally these rocks are dislodged from their orbit, spiral in towards the Sun, and become comets.

Comets are huge chunks of rock covered in ice. As they approach the Sun the ice melts and turns into gas. This streams out behind the comet creating the comet's tail. Although a comet is usually not more than a few kilometres in diameter, the tail can stretch out for over 150 million km.

Comets can reach even more awesome speeds. The fastest comet yet seen was discovered in 1996 and given the unglamorous name of C/1996 S3 Soho. It was a Sun-grazer, meaning it swings very close by the Sun. It reached the phenomenal speed of 618km per second.

Asteroids

These are lumps of rock that orbit the Sun, mostly between Mars and Jupiter.

There may be as many as 100,000 asteroids, most of them only a few metres in diameter. There are only about 50 with diameters more than 160km.

Earth-grazers

Some asteroids pass close to the Earth and are called Earth-grazers. One of them came within 104,000km in 1994. Although it was not much more than 6m wide, it would have caused widespread devastation if it had hit the Earth.

Rocks have hit the Earth in the past. The most recent collision was at Tunguska in Siberia in 1908. It hit the Earth with the power of a large hydrogen bomb and devastated an area 80km across.

Into the infinite

Scientists have detected planets around other distant stars. The chances are that somewhere out there, there are planets like Earth that may also support life. The search for extra-terrestrial life continues, but will we ever find any – or will they find us first!?

Do you want to know what the smelliest thing in the world is, or how hot it can get, or how cold, or the fastest you can go, or the most dangerous thing in the world??? Well, you've come to the right place.

Science is all about why things are the way they are. You'll find lots of other scientific things in this book, stuff about outer space and the Earth.

Here we'll look at the rest of science. From stinky test tubes to incredible powers.

We've got a lot to thank science for. After all you wouldn't have your television or stereo or computer or video games or bike without science.

SPECTACULAR

SCIENCE

1,000,000,000,000,000,000,000,000,000,0

We're going to find out about
- the smelliest smells
- the most powerful forces
- the biggest numbers
- the tiniest bits
- the fastest speeds
- the weirdest inventions

... and some nutty professors!

Fastest speed ever

Light is the fastest thing in the Universe. The speed of light is 300,000km per second. To travel all the way round the Earth and back to you it would take just $\frac{1}{8}$ of a second.

Sound travels at 331m per second – a round-the-world trip would take nearly 34 hours!

See it first

Light is over 900,000 times faster than sound. That's why you see lightning before you hear the thunder.

Sound travels 5 times faster under water and 15 times faster through glass!

GET THIS!

Scientists have managed to slow light down at super-cool temperatures. They've slowed it down to an amazing 60km/h – you could overtake it on a skateboard!

Supersonic

A rifle bullet can reach 3,623km/h or 3 times the speed of sound. Victims are shot by a bullet before they hear it being fired.

Warped speed

Strange things happen if you try and travel near the speed of light. If anyone could see you, they'd see you shrinking. You'd also be getting heavier and heavier. Time would slow down so, if you went on a journey at near light-speed, by the time you got back you'd be only a little older, but everyone else would have died centuries ago.

Happy landing

If you fall out of a plane, the fastest you'll plummet to Earth is about 180km/h – the air stops you falling any faster. Unfortunately, you'd be unlikely to survive.

The furthest anyone has fallen without a parachute and survived is 6,700m. Lieutenant Chisov of the Russian Air Force struck the ground on the edge of a snow-covered ravine and slid the rest of the way. Please don't try this at home.

GET THIS!

The most amazing survival was by Flight Sergeant Nicholas Alkemade in 1944. His Lancaster bomber was on fire and his parachute had burned. He jumped out and fell 5,486m in little over a minute, landed in a fir tree and was thrown into a deep snow bank which broke his fall. He didn't break a single bone!

Atomic

There are something like 10^{85} atoms in the Universe. That's 10,000,000,000,000,000,000,000, 000,000,000,000,000,000,000, 000,000,000,000,000,000,000, 000,000,000,000

or ten sextillion vigintillion!

About 93% of all those atoms are hydrogen atoms.

Atoms are tiny. So, 1 quintillion of them scrunched together would just about cover a pinhead.

The atoms of caesium are the largest of all atoms. If you laid 2 million of them side by side they'd measure 1mm.

Inside the atom are lots of sub-atomic particles. At the centre are a neutron and a proton and whizzing around this nucleus are electrons.

Protons and neutrons are about 1,836 times larger than electrons.

Protons exist for a very, very long time. It has been estimated that the life of a proton is at least 100 decillion (10^{32}) years, or 100,000,000,000,000,000,000, 000,000,000 years, which is considerably older than the Universe.

Now you see it... now you don't

There are 92 elements that occur naturally on Earth. All the others are created artificially.

Seaborgium is so artificial and hates being created so much that it disappears in less than 30 seconds.

Elementary

The first new element to be discovered that was not known to the ancient Greeks and Romans was phosphorus. Hennig Brand found it in 1674 while he was analysing his urine in search of the philosopher's stone.

Aluminium is the commonest metal on Earth yet was not discovered until 1825.

Only 2 elements are liquids at normal temperatures. Yet one of them, mercury, is a metal. The other one stinks so much it is called 'bromine' from the Greek bromos meaning 'stench'.

Gallium is a metal that is used in computers to make them work faster. However, gallium melts if you hold it in your hand. If you squeeze it, it turns to liquid, like ice to water.

Mega-vision

The most powerful microscope is the atomic force microscope which can magnify a million times, enough to see individual atoms.

The Hubble Space Telescope, in orbit round the Earth, is the best optical telescope of all. It can see almost to the edge of the Universe and so back to the beginning of time!

Super-pong

There are 17,000 known distinct smells in the world, and you can produce several of them, some of them very smelly indeed. However, your nose can probably only identify 5,000.

The worst smell in the world is ethyl mercaptan. It's even worse than all your dad's old socks scrunched together. It's the smell produced by skunks. You'd be able to smell it even if there was less than a teaspoonful of it hidden somewhere in your school playground.

Icy cold

The coldest it can ever get is absolute zero. That's −273.15°C.

That's colder than the surface of Pluto, the coldest planet in the solar system. It has a surface temperature of −230°C.

The coldest liquid you can get is liquid helium. Helium turns into a liquid at −268°C which is pretty close to absolute zero.

Liquid helium is weird stuff as it flows uphill!

If you dropped a banana into liquid helium you could shatter it with a hammer.

GET THIS!

It should be impossible to reach absolute zero because at that point all motion ceases, including the movement of sub-atomic particles. However, in 1993 the Low Temperature Laboratory in Helsinki achieved a temperature only 0.28 billionths of a degree above absolute zero. This is colder than the coldest depths of space.

As water freezes it expands. Water expands into ice with a force equal to 140kg per sq cm – enough to squash you flat. That's why frozen water pipes burst.

Whoops

Methane is one of the gases we all produce when we break wind.

It has been estimated that the sheep in New Zealand produce enough methane to meet the entire fuel needs of the country.

A small flock of sheep produces enough methane to power a family car.

Hot, hot, hot

The temperature of your body is about 36.9°C (unless you're ill with flu when it gets a bit higher).

The hottest place on Earth reaches 57.7°C – pretty uncomfortable, but nothing compared with how hot it gets on Venus – 460°C!

The centre of the Sun reaches an incredible 15 million °C but we've actually managed to create a temperature far hotter than that – 510 million °C.

Biggest numbers

A googol is such a huge number it's enough to make you go googol-eyed.

It's 10 to the power of 100 (10^{100}) or

10,000,000,000,000,000,000,000,
000,000,000,000,000,000,000,000,
000,000,000,000,000,000,000,000,
000,000,000,000,000,000,000,000,
000,000.

The figure is so big that the chap who suggested it, Edward Kasner, believes that that many words have yet to be spoken by everyone who ever lived since the dawn of time.

Mind boggling

Kasner created an even bigger number called the googolplex. This is a googol to the power of a googol and is such a big number that there isn't enough space in the known Universe to write it out in full. There certainly isn't enough ink and paper!

The googolplex is so big that from the time the Universe began to the time when all matter decays and the Universe is no more, we will not be even a millionth of the way towards a googolplex number of seconds.

No space for tears

In space astronauts can't cry properly because there is no gravity and tears won't flow. It's quite a job going to the toilet as well! In space water forms into a ball and floats all over the place.

The maddest scientist

Al-Hasen, who lived nearly 1,000 years ago, was a clever but boastful man. He claimed he could control the flooding of the Nile. The Caliph heard of this and hired Al-Hasen to do the job. But Al-Hasen didn't know how to do it, and didn't dare admit this because the Caliph was famous for his cruelty. So Al-Hasen had to pretend to be mad, and keep up the pretence until the Caliph died many years later.

Man's greatest achievement

Injections may not be much fun, but they save a lot of lives. Smallpox was a deadly disease and killed 1 in 4 of those who caught it (and many people did). In 1796 Edward Jenner successfully inoculated a boy against smallpox. In 1967 the World Health Organization began a global campaign of inoculation and by 1980 smallpox had been eradicated – an amazing achievement and the first time any disease had been destroyed.

Big bang

In 1845 the Swiss chemist Christian Schönbein was experimenting in his kitchen at home. His wife had told him not to do this, but she was out. Unfortunately Schönbein spilt some nitric acid and sulphuric acid on the floor. In a panic he wiped it up with the nearest thing to hand – his wife's apron. He then hung the apron over the stove to dry. However, when the apron dried it exploded. Schönbein had discovered nitrocellulose – a powerful explosive. I'm sure it wasn't the only explosion that happened at his home that day!

Learn by our mistakes!

It pays to be untidy. In 1928 Alexander Fleming left some old culture pots full of germs lying about in his laboratory. Some bits of mould fell into these pots and a few days later Fleming discovered the mould had killed off the bacteria. When he examined the mould more carefully he was able to isolate penicillin.

In 1919 Harry Pickup was cleaning out an old ammunitions factory when he dropped some explosive down the toilet. He discovered it did wonders to the dirty toilet, so he went into the toilet-cleaning business!

Whose idea was that?

People invent the strangest things.

Lighter-than-air furniture. Furniture filled with lighter-than-air gases so that when not in use it floats up to the ceiling.

The Whisper Seat. A toilet seat with a special lining so that you can't hear people going to the toilet.

Chewing-gum locket. A container for used chewing gum, to keep it safe in case you want to chew it again.

Chicken glasses. To protect the chicken's eyes from being pecked.

Parrot nappy. A tiny nappy to stop parrots from dirtying the furniture.

Things not worth inventing

- waterproof toilet paper
- cat flap for the fridge
- night-time sundial
- fireproof matches
- toenail glue
- barcode for zebras
- insoluble sugar
- unsinkable anchor
- chocolate saucepan
- indelible soap

Bitter end

Scientific research can get a bit dangerous at times.

In 1626 Francis Bacon had the cool idea that snow might preserve things – like modern fridges do. He leapt out of his carriage on Hampstead Heath, bought a chicken and started stuffing it with snow. (The chicken was dead by the way.) Bacon caught a chill that went to his chest, and he died.

In AD 79 Pliny wanted to study the eruption of the volcano Vesuvius at close hand. He got a bit too close, was overcome by the dust and died.

The Swedish chemist Karl Scheele probably created more new chemical compounds than anyone else. He also had the dangerous habit of tasting them. Amazingly he tasted the highly poisonous hydrogen cyanide and lived. But he also tasted various compounds of mercury, and they got him. He died of mercury poisoning.

MYSTERIOUS

X-FILES

The world is a mysterious place and there are things going on we don't really understand. Have you ever heard things crawling about in your bedroom at night – and there's nothing there!!!???

Have you lost things even though they were there just seconds before? Or seen things you couldn't believe existed – like a clean pair of socks or a £50 note!!!

Have you seen odd shapes in the sky, and they aren't next-door's washing? Or seen strange lights, or ghosts or monsters? Or have you ever dreamed something that later seemed to come true???

I'd better stop before I summon up dark forces. This section looks at lots of those incredible myths, magics and mysteries that we can't explain.

55

Spookiest spots

The title 'the most haunted house in England' was long held by Borley Rectory in Suffolk. For over 60 years there were claims of phantom footsteps and of the ghost of a nun floating around the grounds. The remains of a woman were found in the Rectory in 1943, but no one knows if she was the ghostly nun.

The most haunted village in Britain is allegedly Pluckley in Kent. There are at least 13 different ghosts there including one of the local schoolmaster who hanged himself from a tree. There is also a farm with phantom smells, and a house with phantom whispers!

GET THIS!

The first reference to a haunted house goes back over 4,000 years to the time of the Sumerians.

The most incompetent ghost?

A house in Thetford, Norfolk, was reputedly haunted by a one-legged Jesuit priest. In 1974 police were called to the house when a burglar alarm went off. They were amazed to see a single row of footprints across a room ending at a brick wall. It seems the ghost had vanished through the wall but then set off the burglar alarm!

Ape-men

Are you abominable? Do you have big feet? Maybe you're a Yeti or Sasquatch. These strange ape-like creatures have never been captured but are believed to live in Tibet and remote parts of North America. Some people believe they may be surviving examples of distant human ancestors.

Nessie the slug

The weirdest sighting of the Loch Ness monster was not in the loch but on land. In 1933 Mr and Mrs Spicer saw this globby grey thing wobbling over a road by the side of the loch. They described it as 'a huge snail with a long neck'. Do you think they really saw Nessie, or is there another explanation?

Second time around?

Many people have recalled past lives under hypnosis. One person recalled being the mother of a family of children in Ireland in the early 1900s. She traced the children, who had since grown up, and could remember details of their lives even though she had never met them before.

Vanished!

I bet there are some people you'd like to see vanish off the face of the Earth. It does happen.

All aboard!

The most famous disappearance of all time is that of the crew and passengers of the ship the *Mary Celeste*. This ship was found abandoned in the mid-Atlantic in 1872. There was no one on board, and it looked like the boat had been abandoned suddenly. Although many ideas have been put forward, from abduction by aliens to madness and mutiny, no one knows what happened.

Flushed away

In 1968 Jerrold Potter went into the toilet on a plane while on a flight to Dallas, Illinois. The plane shuddered slightly, Jerrold was never seen again.

Hot air?

In 1881 the MP Walter Powell was carried away in a balloon and never seen again. No debris was ever found of the balloon, the basket or him.

Lost army

In 1915, during the dreadful Gallipoli campaign of World War I, a troop of some 260 men of the Norfolk regiment marched into a wood and disappeared without trace.

Space goblins?

Perhaps the weirdest of all stories about aliens happened in 1955 at a farm in Kentucky. The people living at the farm had to shut themselves in when they were menaced by several small, 'glowing', goblin-like creatures with large saucer-like eyes and arms twice as long as their legs. Bullets fired at these creatures had no effect. It was several hours before the family could escape. Was it a prank, did they make it up, or did it really happen?

The man in the iron mask

From 1669 to 1703 a man was kept imprisoned in France and all that time wore an iron mask. Who was he? Many thought he was the elder brother of the king, Louis XIV, and so the real heir to the throne. It's more likely that Louis XIV was himself illegitimate, and the prisoner a half-brother whom Louis resembled. If this was discovered, Louis would be deposed. Not wanting his brother killed, Louis instead had him imprisoned and his face hidden so no one could see the family resemblance.

GET THIS!

The Dutch psychic, Gerard Croiset, could trace missing people by visions he had when he touched their clothing or possessions. He helped the police track down many missing children. What visions would your old clothes produce!?

Just a coincidence?

When Anne Parrish was in a second-hand book shop in Paris in the 1920s she saw a book of fairy tales she used to love as a child in the United States. When she opened the book she found her name and address inside. It was the very copy she had had as a child.

Two Umberto's

In 1900 King Umberto I of Italy visited a restaurant in Monza and was surprised at how alike he and the restaurant owner were – another Umberto. They discovered they had been born and had married on the same day, and that the names of their wives and their sons were the same. The next day the king learned to his horror that his double had been killed in a shooting accident. As he discussed the tragedy, King Umberto was assassinated.

Unlucky strikes

In 1889 a man was killed in his back garden when he was struck by lightning. About 30 years later his son was killed by lightning in exactly the same spot, and 20 years after that, the grandson as well.

Kaspar the wonder boy

In 1828 a 17-year-old urchin turned up at Nuremberg and started an amazing mystery. He could hardly talk but had letters that said he had been kept all his life alone in a dungeon with a boarded-up window. He could see in the dark and had uncanny powers of smell and hearing. He said his name was Kaspar Hauser.

Mysteriously, he was murdered. No one ever found out who he was or where he came from.

Double trouble

There are loads of coincidences involving twins. Here are just a couple.

Twins born in 1939 were adopted by different families and knew nothing of each other. Yet both were christened James, both had a brother called Larry and a dog called Toy. Both married women called Linda. Both divorced and remarried women called Betty. Both had sons called James. Both worked as petrol pump attendants. Both liked stock-car racing. And both had holidays each year in the same hotel in Florida!

Dorothy Collins lived in Sussex while her twin sister Marjorie lived in South Africa, but both died at the same moment in April 1961.

Miraculous moments

The Indian mystic Sai Baba performs in front of thousands of people, materializing food, flowers and ashes. He lifts himself and others into the air, appears in two places at once and reputedly even raises the dead. No one knows how he does it.

The healing power of the water at Lourdes in France is legendary. Jack Traynor was paralysed in one arm, suffered from epilepsy and could not walk. In 1923 he bathed in the waters at Lourdes and within 4 days was fit and healthy.

Bermuda moped

In July 1974 Neville Ebbin was killed when he was knocked off his moped by a taxi in Bermuda. Exactly a year later, his brother Erskine was killed in the same place when he was knocked off the same moped by the same taxi, with the same driver and the same passenger! How weird is that!?

63

Flaming nuisance

Do your feet sometimes get so hot you think your socks are going to explode? Well that's nothing. Some people suddenly burst into flames. It's called spontaneous combustion. In 1922 Euphemia Johnson was sitting drinking a cup of tea when she burst into flames. Her body ended up as a pile of ashes, but her clothes and the chair she was sitting on were not burned!

Buzz off

Bees have been known to attend the funerals of their beekeepers. At the funeral of Sam Rogers in 1934 thousands of his bees swarmed to the cemetery and settled about his coffin.

What happens next?

Wouldn't it be handy to be able to see into the future? Get a look at those exam questions in advance? Or would you find out something you really didn't want to know?

- In 1812 Countess Toutschkoff dreamed that her father told her her husband would die at Borodino. She warned her husband but neither of them had ever heard of Borodino. A few months later the Count was killed at the Battle of Borodino.

- In 1912 as Mrs Marshall watched a liner steam out of Southampton she suddenly shouted, 'That ship is going to sink!' The ship was the *Titanic*, which struck an iceberg and sank 4 days later.

- The wife of Ulysses S. Grant had a terrible foreboding on the morning of 14 April 1865 and persuaded her husband not to go to the theatre that night. That was the night Abraham Lincoln was assassinated. Apparently Grant was also on the assassin's 'hit list'.

- The night before Exeter in Devon suffered a bombing raid in 1942, hundreds of cats were seen leaving the city as if they knew something terrible was about to happen.

Hover craft

Daniel Dunglas Home was a famous Victorian psychic. He may have been just a clever magician, but one of his 'tricks' has never been explained. In 1868 Home floated out of one window on the third floor and then floated back in another window in the next room! Don't try it – you're more likely to plummet than float!

Predictability

Many people have claimed they can see into the future. One of the most impressive was Jeane Dixon. In 1956 she foresaw the assassination of President John F. Kennedy which happened in 1963. She also had a sudden vision of the death of actress Carole Lombard after they shook hands. She warned the actress not to fly but a few days later she was killed in an air crash.

GET THIS!

Did dinosaurs have guns or have people travelled through time? Some claim that fossils of a few prehistoric animals have been found with bullet holes in them!

FUN AND

What do you like to do when you aren't at school or doing homework or playing with your mates? Watch TV? Play computer games? Read? Listen to CDs? Play football? Shout a lot and run around in circles? Whatever it is, this section covers it.

GAMES

You'll find:
- the oddest sports
- the most daring activities
- the strangest champions
- the noisiest music
- the weirdest books and films
- the fastest games
- the most boring competitions

LET ME GET AT PAGE 70

Head for heights

The longest bungee jump was by Gregory Riffi in 1992 from a helicopter. The bungee rope stretched to over 600m.

GET THIS!

The most spectacular stunt dive was 335m from near the top of the CN Tower in Toronto. It was done by Dar Robinson in 1979 for the film *Highpoint*. His safety parachute opened at 91m, or just 2 seconds before he would have hit the ground!

Snookered

While playing pool, Stuart Russell coughed and his false teeth flew out and went into the corner pocket. When he tried to get them out his arm got stuck and it took 2 police officers, 6 firemen and 50 customers to get him free!

Soccer skill

The fastest a goal has ever been scored in first-class football is 6 seconds. It's happened on 3 occasions, but the first was for Aldershot in 1958.

The highest score ever achieved in a first-class match was 36-0 when Arbroath beat Bon Accord in 1885!

Ball control

Ricardinho Neves kept a soccer ball off the ground by using his feet, legs or head for 19 hours $5\frac{1}{2}$ minutes in 1994.

Keep on running

In 490 BC when the Persians invaded Greece, a Greek, Pheidippides, ran all the way from Athens to Sparta to seek help. The journey was 200km and it took him less than 2 days. He then ran back, took part in the battle, and ran from the battlefield to Athens – another 35km – to bring news of the victory. He ran 470km in 4 days and did a bit of fighting in between. No wonder he dropped dead. The name of the battle? The Battle of Marathon.

Watch out!

How far have you ever thrown, kicked or ejected anything? Could you rival these?

The furthest anyone has ever . . .
- fired an arrow – 1,854.4m – from a footbow
- struck a golf ball – 418.8m
- thrown a spear – 258.5m – from a Woomera
- thrown a frisbee – 200m
- thrown a baseball – 135.9m
- thrown a stone with a sling – 349.7m
- thrown a cricket ball – 128.6m
- thrown a javelin – 104.8m
- thrown a grape – 99.8m – it was caught by someone else in their mouth
- thrown an egg without breaking it – 98.5m – someone catches it!
- kicked a football – 97m
- thrown a cow-pat – 81m – the cow-pat was not fresh
- thrown their wellies – 64m – it was a size 8 boot!
- spat – 29m – spitting a cherry stone

Beat this

The longest any single game has been played non-stop was a game of Monopoly that lasted for 264 hours over Christmas and New Year 1974–5.

In 1974 Gary Martin kept a yo-yo spinning for 55 hours.

The longest any football match has been played, with no substitutes, is 37 hours. It was between 2 American amateur teams in 1975.

Big fight

The longest 2 people have fought each other is 11 hours 40 minutes, in a wrestling match between a Russian and a Finn in 1912.

Tall boy

The highest stilts with which anyone has ever walked were 12.36m high. That's taller than the average house.

Push off

In 1965 Chuck Linster did 6,006 press-ups in just under 4 hours without stopping. The most press-ups in 24 hours is 46,001. The most one-arm press-ups is 8,794 in 5 hours.

On yer feet

The most stubborn endurance event must be the dancing marathon. In 1933 2 dancers survived through a dancing marathon for 3,780 hours, or over 5 months.

Hole in one

The longest distance from which anyone has ever scored a hole in one in golf is 409m.

Basket case

In 1996 Ted St Martin scored 5,221 consecutive free throws in basketball.

Basketball player Wiley Peck slam-dunked a ball with such force that when it rocketed back up from the ground it hit Wiley on the chin and knocked him unconscious.

GET THIS!

The only dead man ever to win a race was jockey Frank Hayes, who died while riding Sweet Kiss at Belmont Park in 1923. He remained in the saddle and was declared the winner before anyone realized he had died.

It's not fair

The 1932 Olympic Games were a bit unfair for some athletes.

- Jules Noël cast a very long discus throw but none of the officials was watching. Noël had to throw again, but produced a much poorer throw and ended up fourth.
- Hilda Strike came second in the women's 100m, beaten by Stella Walsh. However, it was discovered years later that Stella Walsh was actually a man.
- The steeplechase runners had to run an extra lap because the lap official forgot to change the lap counter.

Towers of strength

The greatest weight lifted in a modern competition is 262.5kg, which is equal to lifting 4 full-grown men over your head at once. But there have been other amazing feats of strength.

- In 540 BC, Milo of Crotona, an Olympic wrestling champion, carried a full-grown ox, weighing about 1 tonne, for a distance of 180m.
- In 1891 Louis Cyr lifted 18 men seated on a platform on his back. The total weight was 1,950kg.
- In 1957 Paul Anderson lifted with his back a table laden with heavy metal parts weighing 2,845kg, the greatest weight lifted by a human.

Early champs

The youngest ever world champion was Fu Mingxia of China who won the women's platform diving title in 1991 when she was 12.

The youngest world-record holder was Gertrude Ederle, who broke the 880-yard freestyle swimming record in 1919 when she was 12.

Record records

The best-selling single record of all time is *Candle in the Wind 1997* by Elton John, released at the time of Princess Diana's funeral. It has sold over 35 million copies.

It took 50 years for a single record to beat the previous best seller – *White Christmas* by Bing Crosby, although it's still the best-selling song in the world.

The best-selling album of all time is *Thriller* by Michael Jackson, which has sold over 45 million copies – I bet your mum has a copy!

GET THIS!

The rarest record in the world is believed to be the original pressing of *The Freewheelin' Bob Dylan* (1963). It contains 4 tracks not on the main release and only 2 copies are said to survive. Its value is estimated at around £15,000.

What's the point?

The quietest piece of music is *4 minutes 33 seconds* by John Cage. The title refers to the period of silence during which the musicians sit and listen to the audience.

Groovy babies

The youngest person to have a hit record is Ian Doody, who went under the name Microbe. He was just 3 years old when his record *Groovy Baby* hit the charts in 1969.

The youngest person to have a painting at the Royal Academy was Gino Lyons. His painting *Trees and Monkeys* was painted when he was 3 and exhibited the day before his 5th birthday.

The youngest actor or actress to receive an Oscar was Shirley Temple who was 6 when she received a Special Award in 1934.

The youngest person to have a book published professionally was Dorothy Straight who wrote *How the World Began* when she was 4 – it was published in 1964 when she was 6.

On and on and on

If you listened to all of the music composed by Joseph Haydn just once, non-stop, it would take 340 hours, or over a fortnight. It would take 202 hours, or just over 8 days non-stop, to listen to everything Mozart composed, and 5 days for Beethoven.

The longest piece of music ever performed is the intensely monotonous *Sadist Factory* by Philip Crevier which goes on and on and on for 100 hours.

Fun titles

Here are some fun song titles
- *I scream, you scream, we all scream for ice cream*
- *When there's tears in the eyes of a potato*
- *I've got tears in my ears from lying on my back in bed while I cry over you*
- *If you wanna leave me, can I come too?*
- *Harold the Hairy Ape*
- *Jeremiah Peabody's polyunsaturated quick-dissolving fast-acting pleasant-tasting green and purple pills*

Who's chicken?

One of Glenn Miller's best-known melodies is *In the Mood*. In 1977 Ray Stevens recorded it as the *Henhouse Five Plus Two* with the entire tune made up of chickens squawking.

Loudest music

The noisiest rock concert was the Monsters of Rock concert in 1988. The speakers belted out 250,000 watts of power and the sound of Eddie Van Halen could be heard over 30km away. Wicked!

Suck that hoover

The humorist Gerard Hoffnung composed music for several household objects including vacuum cleaners and kettles.

The Brazilian composer Gilberto Mendes went even further, with music requiring electric shavers, an electric fan, a television set and cups and spoons. How do you think they played the electric fan?

Seriously tiny

The smallest book ever published measured just 1mm by 1mm. It was an edition of the nursery rhyme *Old King Cole* published in 1985. You need a needle to turn the pages.

The shortest record ever released is *The Mistake* by Dickie Goodman which lasts for just 1 second!

What's the point again?

The Nothing Book was full of nothing but blank pages and the film *Sleep* by Andy Warhol runs for 8 hours and just shows someone sleeping.

Perhaps the most pointless hobby was that of Francis Johnson who spent years ravelling together the biggest ball of string in the world. It stood over $3\frac{1}{2}$m high and weighed nearly 9,600kg. How long is a piece of string!?

The letter 'e' is the most commonly used letter in the English language. As a challenge, in 1938, Ernest Vincent Wright wrote a 50,000-word novel, *Gadsby*, without once using the letter 'e'. The only trouble was his name – it had three 'e's in it!

Longest word

The longest word in the Oxford English Dictionary has 45 letters – pneumonoultramicroscopicsilicovolcanoconiosis. It's an illness caused by breathing in fine quartz dust.

Start again!

In 1835, after 5 months of hard struggle, Thomas Carlyle at last finished the first part of *The History of the French Revolution*. He lent it to a friend, and that friend lent it to another friend. That friend left it on a table and the next day the housemaid, thinking it was rubbish, lit the fire with it. Carlyle had no copy. He had to start all over again.

These days, of course, computers can lose entire books in a split second.

Fast work

If you could write as fast as Edward Judson, maybe school would last half as long!

Edward, who created the name Buffalo Bill, claimed he wrote a 610-page book in 62 hours non-stop. That means he wrote at an incredible rate of 1 page every 6 minutes.

Biggest painting

The biggest painting ran on and on for over 3km. It was a panorama depicting nearly 2,000km of the Mississippi, painted by John Banvard in 1846. Unfortunately, it was destroyed in 1891.

Biggest portrait

The largest known portrait was cut into a wheat field by Stan Herd using a tractor! It covered 65 hectares and was a portrait of cowboy film star Will Rogers.

Marvellous models

Ever thought what you could do with your old Coke cans? In 1997, volunteers built a replica of St Peter's Basilica in Rome out of over 10 million empty aluminium cans. It was $\frac{1}{5}$ life size, and stood 29m high.

Syd Darnley of Sydney, Australia built an exact replica of Sydney Town Hall out of 74,000 seashells.

Sandcastle

The world's biggest sandcastle is of Sleeping Beauty's Castle at Pacific Beach, San Diego. It's 12.25m high and weighs 15,000 tonnes.

Worst actor

Fellow actors of Robert Coates in the 1870s demanded police protection to appear on stage with him. At one 'serious' performance Coates, who was always covered in jewels and buttons, refused to leave the stage because he was hunting for a shoe buckle. The audience laughed so much that some needed treatment by a doctor.

Worst orchestra

The Portsmouth Sinfonia, all amateurs, seldom ever hit the right notes or play together. It's often a gamble who'll finish first. Their version of the *1812 Overture* is even more of a disaster than the defeat of Napoleon that it's celebrating – yet people love their performances!

Worst female singer

Elva Miller could never sing in key or in time. Her voice has been described as the sound of 'cockroaches wrestling in a garbage can'. Yet when she recorded her version of Petula Clark's *Downtown* in 1965, it became a massive hit.

Weirdest male singer

Herbert Khaury, better known as Tiny Tim, was a tall, ageing hippy with a high falsetto voice and was once known as the *singing canary*. He had a number of hit records but is best known for his squeaky rendition of *Tip-toe through the Tulips* in 1968.

Worst film

Plan 9 from Outer Space was directed by Ed Wood in 1959. Two aliens try to destroy Earth by raising the dead. Unfortunately the film's star, Bela Lugosi, died before the film was finished. Wood used a double who looked nothing like him – he stayed hidden behind a cloak for most of the film. Wood shot night scenes in full daylight and used car hubcaps and paper plates for flying saucers, clearly suspended by strings.

Movie madness

Here are some crazy gimmicks used to make going to the cinema more fun.

- *Smell-o-vision* – scents were piped into the cinema during the films
- *Horror horn* – a loud horn was sounded to warn the audience of a scary part
- *Quakorama* – seats were fitted with wheels that rocked at the appropriate moments

Who's who?

Some artists change their real name when they become actors or writers. Here's a few where you may understand why they did it.

- Ellen Burstyn was Edna Gilhooley
- Michael Caine was Maurice Micklewhite
- Michael Crawford was Michael Dumble-Smith
- Boris Karloff was William Henry Pratt
- Robert Taylor was Spangler Brugh
- Conway Twitty was Harold Jenkins *(why change it?)*
- John Wayne was Marion Morrison

Million dollar book

The most anyone has ever paid for a book was $30.8 million (£21 million). It was for one of Leonardo da Vinci's notebooks known as *The Codex Hammer* and was bought by Bill Gates, founder of Microsoft, in 1994. What do you think your school books might be worth in 500 years' time?

Comic cash

Collecting comics is a serious business. Some issues are very rare and can fetch quite a price.

Action Comics No.1, £115,600 June 1938 (first appearance of Superman)

Detective Comics No. 27, £103,000 May 1939 (first appearance of Batman)

Marvel Comics No. 1, £71,000 November 1939

Superman No. 1, £81,200 Summer 1939

Batman No. 1, £39,300 Spring 1940

Beano No. 1, 1938 £6,000

Priceless!

The most valuable painting of all is believed to be the *Mona Lisa* by Leonardo da Vinci. It was estimated at £35 million in 1962. Experts are still arguing over who the Mona Lisa was – and what she was smiling about!

Collecto-philes

The biggest collection of marbles numbers over 40,000.

People collect some weird stuff:

- aeroplane sickbags
- beer mats
- bubblegum packs
- cheese labels
- garden gnomes
- light bulbs
- sticking plasters (unused!)

Why, we wonder?

Essential reading

- *Engineering for Potatoes* by B.F. Cargill
- *Learning from Salmon* by Herman Aihara
- *Who's Who in Baton Twirling* by Don Sartellin
- *Enjoy Your Chameleon* by Earl Schneider
- *I Knew 3,000 Lunatics* by Victor R. Small
- *Aliens Ate my Trousers* by Hunt Emerson
- *Captain Underpants and the Attack of the Talking Toilets* by Dav Pilkey

86

ODDITIES AND ENTITIES

Some things are just plain odd, and you'd never believe they were true. Like people who enjoy getting up at 4.00 in the morning, or who enjoy homework!!!

In fact some things are even more odd than that. For the most incredible of the incredible here are some things that defy belief.

Half-baked beans

When police stopped a car in Colchester, Essex, in 1998, they were amazed to find the driver wearing wellington boots full of baked beans.

Barry Kirk, alias Captain Beany, lives his life as a baked bean. He wears an orange jumpsuit and cape and paints his bald head orange.

Lost ticket

When one man went to the doctor about his poor hearing they discovered he had a 47-year-old bus ticket wedged in his ear.

Poopsicles

It's not unusual for frozen poo to fall from the sky. When planes get rid of toilet refuse at very high altitudes it can sometimes freeze and fall as lumps of ice. This usually happens at sea but sometimes they hit land. A Kentucky farmer actually tasted one of these before he realized what it was!

Shock treatment

In the Middle Ages it was believed that ringing church bells would stop thunderstorms. Unfortunately lightning often struck church steeples killing the bell-ringers who were holding on to wet ropes.

Helpful turtle

A young Korean boy fell overboard into the Pacific but was able to climb onto the back of a giant turtle. He was rescued 2 days later.

Master criminals

In 1974 Mrs Sharpe was mugged while she was taking her dog for a walk. The mugger snatched the bag Mrs Sharpe was carrying and drove away. It was only later he discovered that the bag contained dog poo!

In 1985 Christopher Logan, who was on trial for impersonating a policeman, escaped from the court by impersonating a policeman!

In 1989 Stephen Le tried to steal a pick-up truck but was stopped and chased. Le leaped over a fence to escape and then realized he'd escaped into San Quentin prison!

The men they couldn't hang

In 1885, convicted murderer John Lee became famous as 'The Man they Couldn't Hang' when the trapdoor failed to open 3 times at his execution, even though it opened perfectly well when he wasn't standing on it. Instead he was imprisoned for life.

He wasn't the first. In 1803 they tried to hang murderer Joseph Samuels but the rope broke on each of the first 2 attempts and on the third the trapdoor failed to open. Samuels was set free.

Close shaves

In 1901 John Brown was within 1 minute of being hanged for murder when they discovered the wrong name was on the death warrant. Brown's sentence was changed to life imprisonment, but 12 years later the real murderer confessed to the crime and Brown was pardoned.

In 1941 William Wellman was just 2 minutes from death in the electric chair when another man confessed to the crime. Wellman's innocence was later proved and he was released.

Hold your breath

The longest attack of hiccups lasted for nearly 68 years until the victim, Charles Osborne, died in 1990, aged 95. He could never keep his false teeth in.

Super sneezing

The longest attack of sneezing lasted for over 2 years 9 months. The victim, Donna Griffiths, sneezed over 2 million times.

— GET THIS! —

In 1984 Larry Walters thought it would be fun to fly from his garden into his girlfriend's. He tied over 40 helium-filled balloons to a garden chair and shot 4,500m into the air. He was passed by several planes and became a hazard to air traffic. After 2 hours Walters drifted back to Earth but got entangled in overhead power lines, blacking out Long Beach, California! He was arrested and charged with 'flying in a reckless manner'.

What a way to go!

The Greek playwright Aeschylus apparently died when an eagle dropped a tortoise on his head.

Amazing twins

Twin brothers George and Charles can work out the day of the week for any date up to 40,000 years in the past or 40,000 years into the future. They can also remember the weather on every day of their lives. Once when a box of matches spilt open they both instantly said there were 111 before the matches hit the floor!

Speaking clock

A blind girl called Ellen always knew exactly what the time was, to the second, without having access to a clock. She had once listened to the speaking clock over the telephone and had continued to count the time ever after, precisely.

Brilliant babes

Some children display remarkable skills at an early age and are called child prodigies. What's your speciality?

- The composer Wolfgang Amadeus Mozart taught himself to play the harpsichord when he was 3, learned the violin when he was 7, and composed his first symphony when he was 8.
- Anthony McQuone of Weybridge, Surrey, could speak Latin and quote Shakespeare when he was only 2.
- Andragone DeMello spoke his first word when he was 7 weeks old; was playing chess at $2^1/_2$ and graduated from university with a maths degree when he was 10.
- Kim Ung-Yong of South Korea had the highest ever recorded IQ of 210 (150 is 'genius' level). He could speak 4 languages and perform integral calculus before he was 5.
- Jedebiah Buxton remembered all of the drinks he had in his life. When he visited the theatre he counted the number of words each actor spoke.

Raining cats and dogs

Over the years, hundreds of odd things have fallen from the sky. These include:

- live fish
- frogs
- toads
- mussels
- blood
- peaches
- hay
- snakes
- worms
- money

GET THIS!

The greatest known horde of *buried treasure* is believed to be somewhere in the Cherokee Cave of Gold in Whitfield County, Georgia. It was discovered in 1890 by William Waterhouse, who was able to carry out only a few gold bars. But he couldn't find the cave again. The value of the horde is estimated to be about $10 billion.

Truth or myth?

Some stories may or may not be true. They become what are called 'urban myths'.

In New York parents could no longer endure baby alligators as pets so flushed them down the toilet. Now, fully grown alligators live in the sewers under New York.

A man was trying to rescue his cat from a tree and tied a rope to a branch to pull the branch down to ground level. The rope broke, catapulting poor pussy into another garden where a mother and young daughter were praying for a new baby cat!

Now where did I leave my?

Many items of lost property are found on buses and trains all over the world. Some of the oddest held by London Transport's Lost Property Office include:

- a box of false eyeballs
- an artificial leg
- a double bed
- a skeleton
- an outboard motor
- a piano
- a radiator
- a tortoise
- a bidet

Absolutely hopeless

The world's worst army general may well have been Antonio Lopez de Santa Anna, the occasional President of Mexico.

- He was the victor at the Battle of the Alamo, but he lost over 1,500 men.
- After the Alamo he set up camp and ordered his men to take a siesta. They were promptly attacked by the enemy. Santa Anna fled the scene in his pyjamas.
- One clever scheme was to dress his men in the uniform of the enemy, but it all went horribly wrong because no one knew which side anyone was on.
- Santa Anna lost a leg at the battle of Vera Cruz in 1838 but kept the leg with him for 4 years until he was able to give it a state funeral.
- He lost his artificial leg in another battle. Santa Anna had crept away to have a crafty chicken lunch. He was surprised by some American soldiers and fled the scene leaving his leg behind. It's now on display at the Illinois State Military Museum.

Dead loss

The most hopeless suicide may well be Abel Ruiz of Madrid. He threw himself under a train but landed between the lines so the train passed over him. He jumped in front of a lorry but that stopped in time. After treatment Ruiz was talked out of his suicide attempts but upon leaving the hospital he was accidentally knocked down by a horse.

Last post

The longest it's ever taken for a letter to be delivered is 110 years. It was posted in Tennessee in 1863 and was delivered in 1973 to a home for senior citizens in Detroit, where the person it was addressed to had once lived.

---— **GET THIS!** ---—

Legend has it that Jerome Cardano, the noted Italian astrologer, predicted the date of his own death – 2 September 1576. As he neared the appointed time he was still healthy, so he starved himself to death to fulfil his own prophecy.

Puzzling paradoxes

There was a cruel king who arrested every visitor to his land and asked why they had come there. If they told the truth they were set free, but if they lied they were hanged on the gallows. One day a clever-clogs came by and declared that he'd come to be hanged. What could the king do? If he hanged the man, he was telling the truth and should be let go. If he didn't hang him he must be lying and should be hanged!

True or false

Supposing someone says to you 'Everything I say is a lie.' Is he telling the truth or is he lying?

--- **GET THIS!** ---

At least 2 Japanese soldiers did not believe World War 2 had finished. Hiroo Onoda remained hidden in the forests of the Philippines until March 1974 and Teruo Nakamura continued to fight on the island of Morotai, Indonesia, until December 1974. Both believed news of the end of the war was a trick!

Index

a actors and singers 76, 82–3, 84
aliens 59
Antarctic 10, 12, 18, 26
asteroids 41
astronauts 50
athletes 70, 73, 75
atmosphere 24–5, 39
atoms 46

b baked beans 88
bees 65
Big Bang 34
black holes 34
books 76, 80, 84, 85

c caves 14
child prodigies 75, 76, 92
cliffs and canyons 12
coastline 12
coincidences 60, 61–2
collections 85
comets 41
comics 84
continents 10, 16
criminals 90

d deserts 18
dinosaurs 67
disappearances 58–9, 60
disasters 17, 22, 41, 50
diseases 50
dreams 66

e Earth 8–27, 35
earthquakes 19
eccentrics 82–3
elements 46
explosives 50, 51

f fastest things 26, 30, 44
films 83–4
floods 22
football 70–2
future, seeing into the 66–7, 94

g galaxies 30, 31
geysers 21
ghosts 56–7
gold 20

h heat and cold 15, 24, 25, 34, 36, 38, 39, 40, 48, 49
heaviest weights 74
hiccups 91
highest points 14
hopeless individuals 94

i inventions 50, 52
islands 10, 12, 18

l lies 95
light and sound 30, 32, 44–5
lightning 26, 61, 88
light speed 30, 44–5
Loch Ness monster 57
lost property 93

m Man in the Iron Mask 60
memory 57
microscopes and telescopes 47
miracles 62
mistakes 51
models 81
Moon 36
mountains 14, 16
music 76, 77–9, 82
mysteries 56–67

n noisiest things 18, 78
numbers 49

o oceans 14, 20
oddest things 86–95

p paintings 76, 81, 85
paradoxes 95
past lives 57
penicillin 51
planets 32, 38–40, 41
pollution 24
poo and wind 49, 88, 90
postal service 94
predictions 66–7

r rainfall 25
remotest places 12
rivers and lakes 20, 22

s sandcastles 81
Santa Anna 94
science 42–53
slowest things 36
smells 48
sneezing 91
snow and ice 27, 48, 53
space 28–41
space travel 31, 50
speed 30, 35, 44, 45
spontaneous combustion 64
sports and games 70–5
stars 30–2, 34
storms 25–6
strength 74
strongest people 74
Sun 10, 30, 32, 34, 41, 49

t thunder 26
tornadoes 26
treasure 93
twins 62, 92

u Universe 28–41
urban myths 93

v volcanoes 14, 17–18, 53

w water 10, 20, 22, 25
waterfalls 22
waves 12–13
weather 25–7
winds 26, 40
words 80

y Yeti 57